UNDER WHAT

STARS

Poetry by

Ryan J. Davidson

Copyright © 2009 Ryan J. Davidson

All rights reserved. No parts of this book may be reproduced in any way or by any means unless by explicit written permission of the publisher, excerpt for passages excerpted for review and critical purposes

ISBN 13: 978-0-9841025-1-8
ISBN 10: 0-9841025-1-5

Published by Ampersand Books
Ampersand Press, St. Petersburg, FL.
www.ampersand-books.com

Cover design by Ethan Miller

TABLE OF CONTENTS

Leaving or Something Childish but
     Very Natural   …1

The Ramifications of Knowing   …4

Not Written by Candlelight   …5

Gently Confused Smile   …6

Spider-Webbed Streetlights   …7

Pearl Green as a Day   …8

Even the Insects Call for a Reformation   …10

Questions I'll Never ask of the Moon   …11

Having Spent my Time   …12

"The Great Artist is He Who Conquers
     the Romantic in Himself"   …14

Old Women with Flowers   …15

At The End of Every Summer I Wish
     I Had Gone Swimming More   …16

The Words I Owe   …17

Things That Need a Second	…19
Opening The Book	…21
Imperial Palace, Kyoto	…23
How Might I Wake?	…24
Pressing Trees Into Chairs Into Parks	…25
Papers Please	…26
The Nature of the Edge of the World	…27
The River that Carries	…28
Metronome	…29
Another Sea	…30
Burgeon	…31
Pushing Oranges into Light Sockets	…32
At A Young English Poet's Grave	…33
The Perfect Picture	…34
Oranges, Sweatshirts, and Canals	…35

A Father and Daughter	...36
Midnight Sounds Every Hour	...37
Flowers' Names	...38
That Bottle Has No Label	...40
Not So Long Ago	...41
Postcards from A About Her City	...43
Up-State Trying to Hold onto What's Left of My Left Atrium	...44
To The Girl I Deceive Daily	...45
Shaking Trees to Loosen Leaves	...46
My Elevator Smells Anonymously Feminine	...47
Where I Find Myself	...48
The Living Breathing Poem	...49
Walked Out on Me	...50
In a Café, Almost Alone, At Dusk	...51

Pavlov's Dogs	…52
The Cherry Blossoms are Blossoming	…53
In The Rain There are Still Candy Machines	…54
A Flower in the Throat	…55
Sweating Like a Turtle	…56
The Start of November, Columbus Circle, New York, New York	…57
After a Russian Poet	…58
Missed Connections	…59
Postcards to _____	…74

My beloved who wills not to love me:
My life which cannot love me:
I seduce both.

-Jack Kerouac

LEAVING OR SOMETHING CHILDISH, BUT VERY NATURAL

I want to burn bridges and block
       every tunnel with my voice.
To tell you how much you should stay,
       how you're my sun and my moon—
       if only watery sentiment would work.

What good are words?
Just more idle things that leave
me here speaking to no one.

In my sleep, still here,
       you right next to me;
       your head rested in sex-ripened headrest.
If I could just show you,
       by pointing at the place in my head
       where I remember walking to the window
       and looking at a sunrise while holding you naked,
       then my fingers wouldn't have to dance this
       keyboard.

I never thought ill of talking to myself,
       but talking to rocks gets grating.
Words found furlough between your ear and my tongue,
       prisoners of interpretation allowed to play baseball
       outside when it was nice enough,
       like those bedraggled souls in Comstock.
It seems life was hidden underneath sofa cushions,
       and within those arm encircled sunrises.

Awestruck hearts left stumbling within,
       and without, a stanza
       seeking meaning to give life to dead ideas,
       like God,
       that still exist only in the starched Sundays of
       devout followers.

My lips stumble punch-drunk and fat
       as I try to shape truths from doughy thought.
The only certainty I've found is that days don't pass quick
       enough when they are Great Wall in-between now
       and when I again hold you, and feel your body
       pressed into mine;
reminding me of crumpled paper
       and the uselessness of silhouettes
       to represent emotion,
       and how many times I crumpled
       paper to fix sentiment.
If the first poets could scratch their horses
       and hunts into cave walls
       I'll use what they left
       to show what keeps me alive,
       though it feels, at times, like a
       paper rose on an anniversary.

About now is when you'd call me home
       or to you, all I hear though is the trill of thrushes
       tinged with lustful memories of the sea.
       If you could hear them you'd swear
       they were saying your name.

If every brushstroke is a word on canvas,
     and each word overlaps to create the perfection
     of cubic zirconium
     it will never equal the vignettes conjured
     by a lexis simple as love.
Perspective always points to a painting's nowhere,
     so I paint pictures with shadowed ink
     and my own philosophy
     in hope of learning a broader perspective than
     eyelashes.

THE RAMIFICATIONS OF KNOWING

I've been away for years,
quietly mapping my American sub-conscious
from an expatriate perspective,
and learned that if it's snowing anywhere it's always here.
And that a plan is really just a list of things that won't happen,
on top of a million other idiotic Hollywood idioms,
but no one explained the value
of solitary nights on a bed in Mexico.

I remember last glimpses
and a hundred sad goodbyes
but not a single hello,
      or one daisied face to put with the list of names.
I remember sex poems,
      and the moist warm swampish feel of them
      but not the soul-talk
      they should be predicated on.

I picture how much time is really in 1,221,600 seconds.

Clocks are just an idea until their hands are holding you back.
Distance is concrete and I miss it.
The earth is telling stories in each crunching step.
At night when the crush can resound
      from brick building to brick building
      I hear it telling me to run till I'm surrounded by cement
and have seen the halo of streetlights,
      and been inches from their aspirations.

NOT WRITTEN BY CANDLELIGHT

No quicker will people call you crazy
than when you scream created names,
like God, in the cold of sleep.

I write by computerlight to see whether
I can put blind words onto paper in search
of the similarities between binary and brail.

Like the first logic machines read holes
I read India ink on night colored pages in search
of the similarities between technology and religion.
For me the quiet hum of computerlight
promises sex, knowledge, and understanding.

Meaning in the world is oxygen; it's there,
it's everythere, but it's impossible
to push a pin into it.
One word, or just a line, shapes meaning
like a glance can decide the future, or one night.

Candlelight usually represents truth,
except when it drips like watery sentiment.

GENTLY CONFUSED SMILE

That look like they know the feel of my hands
and I'm supposed to smile back at them.
I sit in a room and think about
the quiet way the chair's legs merge
with the floor, like the threads of a spider web,
to remind us we're balanced on an egg, of sorts,
as if we'll see anything outside of our eye-lashes.

I'm starting to understand the importance
of a local, an American idiom and now.

SPIDER-WEBBED STREETLIGHTS

He meant only to kiss her shoulder
but decided this was a kicking-a-small-
child idea. As he had committed
to an action he closed his teeth

around his favorite of her angles
to fill-up what, otherwise, would've been
a useless movement of his head closer to hers.
If you had seen the look
in his eye, the left one she said

twinkled with the reason he went to three high schools
like a frozen waterfall threatening to re-cataract,
you would've seen that he knew he'd gone too far
before he bowed his head and she ran again.

Miscarried actions don't translate.
He wonders whether they ever spoke the same tongue.
He remembers the picture of fishnet stockings with one
hand surreptitiously tugging the edges she pasted
into the crafty book he scribbles in—and realizes: no one
ever spoke so closely with so many mirrors in-between.

PEARL-GREEN AS A DAY

I wonder what needle-filled promises Baudelaire would
find in her burnt-ice eyes waiting in lonely rooms
that ring with chain-on-chain clink.
Where would he quietly eviscerate her with verses
he had composed with just that in mind,
leaving each *je t'aime* a little sharp?

The thought:
Of other words tumbling through the sheets,
caressing her tongue with their perfectly formed forms,
Of other poetry passing through her ear,
to rap gently on the hammer and anvil, clicking rhythm,
Of her loving other writers never bothered me
until I heard a tone I thought reserved for me in her voice.

Would Hemingway have made her
a pretty thought,
or a walk in the rain?
I can see the terseness with which he'd make every
"What about the Pound-cake of Paradise?
Don't you wonder what it tastes like?"
conversation we had seem so conjunctive.

I know she'll read others, and see others,
and probably fall in love like a writer falls in love—
having something to do with the imagination—
but trains still to be ridden gnaw
at the edges of old newsprint,
and I'm left ragged at the corners.

I wonder how Kerouac would rant through the edge
of her jaw, or if he'd see the road in her smile too.
The electricsounds of her head as she reads his work
picturing the bluenote that he heard when he wrote it,
      and feeling what the magnetic railway and his
mother meant.

EVEN THE INSECTS CALL FOR A REFORMATION

She asked me to:
"make [her] want to write." I

want to put a muse under her eyelids
and each of her fingernails.
I want to put the noise of
insects that are too loud into a melody

I can fill her lungs with, just
by putting my finger to her lips.
She sees me as dead and my
bed as a grave. I feel
the words we made each other spit out

and can recite more of them
than I'll admit. There is a dead clock
in the corner who watches her think
but that moment will wander off
to take another picture; the clock hopes she'll
wind up in foreign-family

albums. I look at old photos
and name those moments now.
She reminds me, by burrowing into the headrest I
create when I make my shoulder
into the space between a violin's beaks,

of the way her hand twitches, or used to,
as she begins to fall asleep.

QUESTIONS I'LL NEVER ASK OF THE MOON

I've been building my own moon,
using scraps of conversation for the surface
and things not said for craters
and canyons,
but I managed to see the real moon

and I must begin
again; it rained on my way home.
I lost sight of the proper
moon, and pulled over, not to wait

out the rain but to think of honesty,
and how I lied to her when she guessed
what it was I wanted to ask—
back to paper, plaster,

and water. Every time she appears, having un-swaddled
herself, she remembers another girl with a gravity
that makes it seem as if there is another infidelity
coming every tomorrow I can conceive

of. And what about
a future of imperfections?

Now I see the darkened
part of the moon where it could
be black
and I think she lied when she answered
a question I didn't ask.

HAVING SPENT MY TIME

Cherry blossoms fall away
from happiness. It seems
they think there is more
to come in their next incarnation.
There is a description
to be shown, through these blips:
the way a hand feels
as its phantom brushes my arm
while I wake. I reach out—

hours imply contentment; seconds
allude to impatience. Months, though, months
are ripe with sardonic laughter. I almost choke
on time as if I've forgotten how to breathe
or am suddenly allergic to air.

One of the things worth believing in,
either air or time,
has me by the carotid. I aspire
to the grace of cherry blossoms,

but I don't want their faith in fate. This smells
of spring: the thick ozone taste
of more impending rain, the earthy smell
of drowned worms murdered by
the flower's life. Birds are busy stealing
to decorate their homes, the sun
starts to cook my face when I turn it up
in recognition of the day, my heart beats slower again.

I reach out—to grab hold of air or time
but like light they slough away.
I think of 432 days as a road,
as a narrow road to the far north,
where skins can be shed
so nerves will touch more closely. Hours
are meant to be traveled
through, the destination, though, is old.

"THE GREAT ARTIST IS HE WHO CONQUERS THE ROMANTIC IN HIMSELF"

-Henry Miller

When I was 12, for no reason,
I had a pair of silk-leopard-print boxers;
this isn't my childhood—
more like the infrared end of the spectrum.

If I knew what I wanted
to say I might be able to bring together a
tombstone to scrape the edges of a scab
that won't scar over—I might be able
to make a story.

Now feels like
someone reached into
the mouth of time, grabbed
its tonsils and pulled so hard
my digital clock only reads
in mirrors. Though I've forgotten
the old-language I can't put metaphors
together in the new one. Neither
seemed able to do the job of explaining
morning clouds, cut through with sun,
roiling over mountain tops in the North of Japan
and what the sight does to the insides of my eyes.

It was my birthday and I realized:
all my underwear are cotton and most
are only one color now.

OLD WOMEN WITH FLOWERS

At the bus stop there are two old women
wearing black, or at least dark, clothes
with matching black, or at least dark, hats.
One woman wears glasses the other
carries herself as if she needs to.
They both clutch flowers.

The women seem to have just given
birth to those bobbly-headed flowers.
They have that hand grip—the one
where one arm supports the head
and the middle and the other creates
a rail—but it looks less
precarious with the flowers. I think
the women's necks are craned, impatiently.

AT THE END OF EVERY SUMMER I WISH I HAD GONE SWIMMING MORE

I just thought of gardens,
a patch behind an aunt's house
that I only ever remember
like you see a building through a snowstorm.

With that thought I'm washed in hospital
air. I wish there were more
flowers to give. Instead I have the honesty
that scrapes off my teeth in the morning.

It's the care more than the flowers that I remember.
When I was young I wanted to learn the names
of every plant, now the colors will do. I only know
one name: Tulip. This works for all of them since
they never come when you call them anyway.

THE WORDS I OWE

The thing is: it's still day anywhere,
even imprisoned in a new womb
waiting to see what sort of karma waits
on the other side of divine vulva.

How proud X would be
if she saw all the toppled buildings I've
left in my wake, just this once—
for the sake of modernity
and literalism—I'll call it a jet-stream.
A Japanese snow-flake, an actual

snow-flake not a metaphor, danced…
No, cantered before my face; sauntering
the circumference of my humbled head.
Personal gravitational field is an explanation;
I prefer to think it was judging my symmetry.
As it finished its circuit it paused before my mouth

and I held my breath. Then sharply in, and I had
broken it against my two lips.
I smoke constantly in honor of the scents

I no longer wish to contain. I wonder
about days; the laundry pile they create
stuffed next to my door—dirtied pants
mixed with soiled time. Mornings seem
covered in messy red during-birth
like truth and the slop it brings with it.

For today I'd like to smile,
and see the girl with the hips
walk through my wall again.

THINGS THAT NEED A SECOND
After Keats' "Ode on Melancholy"

Your breath to become
a frosted puzzle of crystals
when blown onto a cold-
window from inside. Regretting
something stupid you say
to someone whose picture
of you probably doesn't matter
as much as the cigarette-smoke
still
              trailing
after
                        the
                                    last
          word.
Eye-contact with a stranger
whom you hope will wear that smile all

day for the microwaved moment you shared.
Train-doors to close and take away dice that are
still turning. Reading the last word
and punctuation mark of a new favorite book.

The wave's rainbow which we'll
turn to a child's smile when they learn
they can make them at home
with their thumb and a hose.

Getting your nose broken. Crashing
a car. Perfume going from perfume

to a kind of gravity. Getting comfortable
with flowers. These things aren't death,
beauty, or time—just, all the same,
things to washout with wine.

OPENING THE BOOK

> *"What is that feeling when you're*
> *driving away from people…*
> *it's the too-huge world*
> *vaulting us, and it's goodbye."*
> *-Jack Kerouac*

Sitting on the train after she had to say good-bye
to me even though she was the one leaving,
I opened <u>On The Road</u> since it's arriving and leaving,
and as close as I've gotten to feeling both at the same time.

I spent an hour reading a new river because
I can't afford to drink and found "The Poetry Path,"
but it was too dark for me to wander
down. I'll do more; I always do more tomorrow—
except on Mondays; the museums are closed on Monday.
On those days I tend to just meander—from
coffee shop to park to coffee shop—
too tired to work too young to feed pigeons.

I still think she'll be somewhere
when I get back, though I'm not sure where,
but there's something in knowing she's somewhere.
All I have are my own two eyes.
All I have is a Northern Tohoku night
building itself over the skeleton of another
day whose only purpose was to threaten
rain, and I wish I could see how Tokyo feels when she
leaves it, all I have are my own two eyes though.

I'll see her face every now and again,
in fogged mirrors, my own ghost
of the young woman Mary
but comfortable like a hotel bible.

IMPERIAL PALACE, KYOTO

These places—where leaves hold
the wind and the buildings strive
to out-shine the sun they live with—
are meant for the study of habits.

There's a knot of 450 birds above my head—
a floating forest in this panicked-
jubilant state; since the sky is still blue it looks
like pieces of night are trying to create evening
by slamming into one another.

Not many people speak intelligibly
here but I hear hungry birds
cry out in something of a symphony
and "outsider" repeats like a dog's bark
from every third person that passes.

One couple stops to look
at Charlie Brown's foliage-tree.
They smile at the tree and each
other and the tree again and walk
away, still holding hands.

HOW MIGHT I WAKE?

When others sleep, while the sisters,
fathers, mothers, brothers,
sons and daughters in our infinities rest,

this is the moment we see, without
the periscope of participation, how much smaller
our childhood fields have grown. Another effort
spends my time and I'm sick with
it. There's always more to say but I can't get
the night's colors right (I wish

I could paint less like a child).
There's a fuzz that coats my teeth
like morning breath; it comes out
in the nightmares and the dreams
I remember all the same.
People may not be able to conceive of the end
but we think constantly of what has
come before: that snake eating itself

can see little of itself. No body,
no head, maybe the scales of its tail.
I've heard her speak of sleep and
I can see pictures of her waking up, the pain
of closing her eyes and her nightmares—
the color of sheets. These things have

let me into a bedroom where I press my
lips to a neck in lieu of kisses.

PRESSING TREES INTO CHAIRS INTO PARKS

I'd like to make something with my hands,
something out of wood and nails,
that I can point to with a half-smile and,
even though it wobbles a bit,
say, "that's a truth and I put it there."
It's draining to fall in love every few days,
so I think of Prague and use my eyes
to make trees into chairs—for now. The river is still

still, but I can't find a time
when my pulse doesn't pound.
Parks should be meadows dotted with trees
where the grass sways to my iambic heart.
Because it's almost cold again
parks are boats rocking against
the wind. In magic there's that moment,
just before the card is produced,
when you focus like something's about to be born,
this is the way three days
have felt: like a card is waiting.

PAPERS PLEASE

"It's only an hour of my life," seems
enough at the start but as things turn Novocain
I lose some of the security-blanket warmth along

with the feeling. *Papers please*, things that
can be checked, verified: passport,
driver's license, citizen number—
agreed-upon facts. I can tell you:

where I've been, girls I've smiled at,
which smiled back, how often I've seen
the tides turn on the Atlantic and the Pacific,
how many cigarettes I smoke in a day,
where I'm from—most of this won't hold up
against my papers. It's only an hour
of my life, *papers please*. If anyone asked me
where I'm going I might say "nowhere"

but just as affectation; I think I left home
to go home to start a new home,
or something equally improbable. *Papers please*.

THE NATURE OF THE EDGE OF THE WORLD

When I came back to life this morning
my head was split open and my mouth
felt like I'd been chewing lizard eggs
wrapped in tar-paper, so I went to stand
on the deck of the boat carrying me
to Russia. A hangover is basically
dehydration; "water, water everywhere
and not a drop to drink." In this vein

I thought of people who drowned,
by drunkenness, bravery
or cowardice and, eventually,
the ocean. At night,
stumbling the aft deck, drunk on vodka
and beer I, like Li Po, want to embrace the moon;

not that I want to drown, but the
moon's reflection seems so convenient.
This is why I can't write about the ocean—
there's too much left.

THE RIVER THAT CARRIES

The wakes of passing boats
carry the music of those
with more money than sense
to the shadow of The
Citadel. I think I'm

watching the time pass
when I'm actually making
it (I'm sorry this is only
in English; I'd write
in every language if I
could). Today I walked
from shade to shade

trying to make life easier than
the calculus I created.
Drinking a red Hungarian
night trying to forget

the misplaced kisses
(Amazing how many in one
day). The music, to spite
the day, makes us dance a little.

METRONOME

Where Stalin stood there is now
a 60 foot metronome and rock music
pumping out of speakers I can't see.
Beautiful should be the same in
every language. I miss being naked.

The metronome reminds me that
nothing is outside of time.
There is a view from the tip of the ever-
enduring now but I'll keep the picture
for my memory of Prague.

ANOTHER SEA

I keep thinking about how the sun
felt on my face at one a.m., and know
this is a tarot card. I used to have a cast
on my hand from when I tried to knock
down a building, a friend wrote "love" on it;

now I have a calcium deposit where it broke;
nothing really just a feeling, when you rub
the skin on the back of my hand, of more being

added to less. My train turned into a boat—
I guess to remind me how important
water is—the hull split like a
water-logged melon and the train
nestled into the hold
for the trip across the sea between Germany

and Denmark. I guess, as long as we get
where we want, sunsets
can remind us of kaleidoscopes.

BURGEON

Burgeon is not,
contrary to the reasoning
that might lead you
to believe this to be so,
a portmanteau
for a pigeon
which is a burden;
it is when something
begins to grow.

PUSHING ORANGES INTO LIGHT-SOCKETS

The Forum tastes of morning breath,
        of an electrical socket, of a soft
        slightly upturned breast that
        I haven't tasted yet, of a fresh orange.
Instead of remembering
        that "free radical" isn't a revolutionary term
        I'll try to remember what the yellowed moon
        looked like as it set into the Tiber river—
        the smell of the breeze
        that blew off the forum—
        and the look of that Irish girl
        who liked me more than I do.

AT A YOUNG ENGLISH POET'S GRAVE
After "At Apollinaire's Grave" by Allen Ginsberg

I came to Rome to find you here,
  buried where you died like a sailor drowned at sea.
All these flowers and a pyramid as backdrop
  don't seem like your name was "writ in water."

I stumbled into The Protestant Cemetery holding my own hands
  because there was no one there, and because
  there's comfort in touching something you know.

I entered as a desert, with one sandy
  dune pushing against the other.
Watching your stone bounce sun-rays I thought of names
  written with embers in open air and those carved
  in water, but mostly of where I'd sleep.

I envy you your history left in stone;
  people died quicker in your day;
  candles don't flicker when snuffed.
I read your letters;
  I read them even though they weren't to me;
  your handwriting is squashed spiders
  but the words are fireworks bursting above The
  Colloseum.

I hope you picture me a pilgrim
  thinking of my Fannie Brawnes
  on the bench by your stone.
A gravestone marks our last meeting;
  I want to be buried so your shadow touches my grave
  and sit with our stones to watch them grow mold.

THE PERFECT PICTURE

A three or four year old boy with the same camera
I have (his parents must've bought it for him
so he could play the tourist, too)
stood outside the Italian *Macina E scrive*.

While his father took a picture of the typewriter
the boy took a picture of two half smoked cigarettes
in a corner, behind a chain. And I admired
him, and wished I had more film.

ORANGES, SWEATSHIRTS, AND CANALS

The green in the canal water of
Venice reminds me of her
sweatshirt. They're not the same but
one reminds me of the other
the way an orange still tastes like
the Roman Forum covered in sun. There's a word for that,
when one thing comes to stand for another...
I learned the word once.
Now, though, I've lost it. Small points

equal bigger ones: "Come to Verona for the night,"
J said. I lied: "no, I don't have my ticket." She
left and I watched another train disappear. In no rush I sat,
        sitting,

I watched the sun set behind the Venice train station
and wondered about passports, middle-names
and what I would have for breakfast. When I left America
I knew what my house looked like and that I'd
usually eat dinner. I've lost these certainties now; instead
I have this green sweatshirt with full-zip
and a hood that lives behind my eyes, I haven't seen it

in a year and a half, but I thought of its green
watching the canals sway this evening.

A FATHER AND DAUGHTER

After his daughter tried unsuccessfully
to place on his working-fingers her
pink-plastic-bead ring, the father held it in his hand,
made fist, and said, I imagine, "which hand?"
She giggled, guessed right, squealed
with pleasure - slightly - then smiled at me.
When we passed a daisy field I pointed to it

and she smiled at it too. This girl is
a part of my new mythology now;
I wonder if she'll remember me
as long. Probably she'll think of the drunken-Irish boy
snoring in a sleeping bag on the floor
next to us. It's a matter of sleep more or less.

MIDNIGHT SOUNDS EVERY HOUR

"But how did it feel to travel that far?"

It felt of: Cash machines that don't work—ever,
tombs, bridges that only rise at night,
a museum full of cartoons and hand-made radios,
concentration camps, a woman holding a palm
frond over her head in victory forever,
a beach made of pebbles from buildings
America blew up, a castle, a wall—
or pieces of outdated ideologies,
an ineffable green, a beddish park,
a Stalin-sized metronome, a brothel and a prostitute,
twelve-dollar cigarettes, a bed like a sunny park,
the Eiffel tower seen through hair blown against my face,
a plaque for T.S. Eliot and my family.

A letter I haven't finished writing is waiting for me
at my grandmother's house in Scotland
in an envelope covered in Russian stamps; though
I went half-way around the world, it wasn't
to finish this poem.

FLOWERS' NAMES

I thought, not so long ago,
I'd like to learn how to call that flower.
By "not so long ago" I mean four months.

I have pictures and a book,
it's the movement that's gone.

Being fall now there aren't many flowers left
to call anything, most gardens are just
empty houses without even dust-covers.

The cornices, gilt windows, statues, squirrels,
girls that look like The Venus of Willendorf

and boys who traditionally look
as if they need a shower are all the family
I need. There are three tiers of seats; I am

in the third not because I'm scared,
of hands pressing my shoulder

(I am) or eyes seeing the state of my clothes,
(I am) just that I want a larger field of vision—
something god-like about watching people pass

or stand beside you—
without them noticing you.

Days are chunks of orange to wrap your lips
around, to remind you of where you've been
and concerns from before time was a concern.

What time is it?
Now, now, or now?

THAT BOTTLE HAS NO LABEL

I know what every sign means;
not to say that I can read them;
they're more than games
of Boggle now. I held mystery

like a suitcase while I
wandered and learned not to be
embarrassed to tell people "I'm
a poet." I still don't know what to say

when asked if I'm any good
though. Instead I tell them "I fell in love
with a lesbian" and they seem to understand
that more than "yes" or "no."

I want more from me than my withered old woman
soul has the hands to weave, and because I say
"I'm shy" I'm actually growing to it.

Now, I fall in love with streets named after women.

NOT SO LONG AGO

-6 Months Ago-
"We've walked for two hours,
let's sit down here" she said. It rained
while they sat in front of a miniature
field of yellow tulips. Each time the wind
blew the tulips bowed to the statue
at the head of their box. She
fingered the toe of her shoe and smiled
while she spoke. "What's this park's name?"
she asked. "It's called Peace Park.
Are you ready to keep going?"
they were going to the beach to see
what was left of the snow in Aomori.
Through the park and stopped again in front of a clock
with its own sea of yellow tulips in a circle—
mouths open wide in anticipation of the hour.
They waited for the hour too, mouths closed
except for talking. The clock had a statue
on top, an iron seesaw, with two iron kids—
that weren't kicking or laughing.
"It should do something on the hour;
let's wait and see," she said and scuffed
her shoe along the pavement.

-6 Months Later-
"It's so great you're back," she says.
He asks, "when can I see you?"
She answers "I wrote you a poem about that
day in the park." They stood
in the rain, a rain like the water that comes
out of an open shower curtain, for an hour
and a quarter.

In my head she's folded up
holding the bottom of her left foot
and the phone with her other hand.

POSTCARDS FROM A ABOUT HER CITY

No one told me about New York—
not Whitman, Ginsberg, Ashberry—nothing
I can taste with my fingers. I've under-

taken an effort to see more.
I'm hoping Lorca's visions
will stop me from drinking so much that
people ask "why do you drink so much?"
I have nothing to say about lights. I've barely
seen them, just a sky pink all night to conceal the stars.

Because I can't stop remembering The Brooklyn Bridge
I'd like to see it, that's next and next.

I'm reading a woman I don't know and, sexy
as she is, I think of her as 62 constantly. Chunky lines
and stanzas set in form to preserve,

sonnet as amber. I have no new smiles
but the old ones are coming back to me,
new cities that gleam with promised bottles
of red-wine, the girls who laugh spring-time, a
new word that means more than "me," these are not
the formations of muscular contrac-
tions; these are the stories of smiles; I think
this is because I've sown my sunglasses
into the bed. Not to let the sun in,
so that people can see my eyes look at/
for the sun and yellow umbrellas. It
might be cold again, I won't say I'm work-

ing with the honest part of my character
though I've smiled most of the day today.

UP-STATE TRYING TO HOLD ONTO WHAT'S LEFT OF MY LEFT ATRIUM

I can't tell stories;
the only ones I have are true
and people can't believe them.

They all tend to be "and nothing happened.
We just shared a bed." Or "before I left
we sat together on the tailgate of her truck
and kissed while I told her 'this'd be more perfect
if I were the captain of a football team'.
She laughed and said 'then I'd be a cheerleader'."

TO THE GIRL I DECEIVE DAILY

I guess overall she's in me.
Every time she asks
if we'll meet someone I say yes,
and when, on those rare occasions,
we do she asks: "are we going to be true?"
(in the sense of a dog, a pregnancy test, and math)

I say yes. I never mean it.
Rather, I mean it but forget it
by the time the litmus test
comes around. There are no new shapes
in any of this. So today,
which means nothing to you,

on my back, wet-close
to a fountain, with my head
in another lap, I thought of love
stories, but I felt not even a funny-bone
of guilt when the lap girl asked the me-girl
what I was thinking and she answered
"we should've done this more."

SHAKING TREES TO LOOSEN LEAVES

No one wants to buy my
"sometimes the best way to not drown
is to not swim" much less "I saw a man today on 3rd
and 33rd shake the leaves off a tree
so he could clean them up." When I eat oranges

I think of the forum, when I think of eating oranges
I picture the canals in Venice, a woman named
the world and our ability to train connections.
I kissed her on stairs to nowhere while
tourists took photos of us, or the stairs. Tonight,
which means nothing to you, back in New York
I watched rats dance around subway tracks,

even as the train wheels crashed towards them.
One of the rats, I reckon it was a woman

but how do I know, rushed at the train
as the train rushed at her.
When I die I'd like to be cremated;
I spent my whole life smoking. I'd like

to be scattered on The Charles Bridge in Prague.

MY ELEVATOR SMELLS ANONYMOUSLY FEMININE

I was thinking, moments ago
standing on my balcony
overlooking the west side of Graz,

how easy it is to write
vaguely. To say her, him,
they, even you (but "you"
usually addresses the reader).

I say M, G, E,
you see whomever you
(you the reader) want. How
could you see my girlfriend,
bank teller, or the server
at my local café?

After so many
"Lauras" you're just
meant to understand that Laura
is the perfection of cubic

zirconium. Don't start reading
again looking for this Laura;
she isn't here. I knew a Laura
but not in that way and it was
a long time ago. I'm happy enough
with her and you for the moment.

WHERE I FIND MYSELF

Where I wake up has been mathematic.
Strange to think how little
changes with the continents.

Abstracted ideas of love and beauty
are just to burn calendar pages
but Humpy Dumpty's linguistics
alleviate the ache I'm pressing
into me with folded arms. My drinking
is just enough, so long as I can think
of words tangible enough
to wear the scarf I made to pull them together.

Did I tell you I saw the white cliffs of Dover?
When I saw them, though, they were orange
with the warning lights of spires, antennas,
and too tall buildings. I suppose
that poem has already been written.

THE LIVING BREATHING POEM

It seems like beautiful art always references
April, but they can keep their sunny-swampy
corpses. Mid-September to early October
is the darkest time, not a metaphor.
Something about the days growing shorter
makes me want to shave more often. In spite of,

or because of, all the tricks I try, I keep finding myself
hurt in new and interesting ways. Yesterday,
thinking of Big Wheels and dodge-ball, I rolled down
a far too steep hill. When I stopped I stuck my hand
into glassy gravel and came up with a new color of
blood (I'll call a grayish-red.) spattered
across the inside of my palm.
My head has almost stopped burning

from where it met a fist. This seems a good sign that
telling someone "I love you" will correct not actually
loving them, but I wonder if the inverse will find
itself as well. My head has almost
stopped hurting; that's enough for today.

WALKED OUT ON ME

On waking this morning, *sans*
hangover, there was a girl in bed
next to me. She turned out to be
imaginary but this was only after
she boiled water for coffee,
shared my morning cigarette,
and kissed me well.

She puttered around a kitchen
that looked like mine in a way
that meant it wasn't. Dreaming
dreams I didn't have last
night but had heard about
over coffee I had yet to drink—
I walked out on her.

It was early, she didn't have class
and I didn't have to walk home.
I smiled to myself all morning
until the teeth started to fall
out of my mouth.

IN A CAFÉ, ALMOST ALONE, AT DUSK

The quiet of a wrecked ship—
the only sound the murmur
of speakers with no music
left to play; I'm sure
if there were music it'd be
Italian arias played from LP's.
I'm not sure how

much I'll have, but while it's here
I'll drink as much of it
as I can get a good hand on.
I've been thinking of the sea

and trips I've made.
The whole ocean
comes unwound at the
touch of Whitman's sweaty poems.
I always picture him as uncontrollably
nervous, almost shaking.

PAVLOV'S DOGS

We were sun-dials at night
when we heard the click-click-click
of a woman running towards us,
like a ball bouncing through
a roulette wheel. We both

turned to look. I didn't know why. T
said "I love the sound of a woman

running." When I pushed for
an explanation he answered
"the sense of anticipation."

THE CHERRY BLOSSOMS ARE BLOSSOMING

On my little piece of street,
the one I can see from the new window
of my new apartment I moved into after my
newly-old girlfriend threw me out for sleeping
with someone else, the trees are screaming,
losing their minds, making beauty
and throwing it away. The white blossoms
fall away like the skin on my hands
when I work them too hard cutting down trees.

In Japan, at the *Hanami* festival,
underneath trees—watching flowers—
I figured out the blossoms
have a faith in fate I'm trying to learn.

People watch the pink, red, and white petals
dance in the afternoon sunshine, with friends.
They sit on blankets, talk, and drink.
someone is supposed to recite a haiku.

I would work my fingers like
I was practicing the piano trying to count
out those limits. I made one in my head once,
said it, forgot it and felt more like the flowers.

IN THE RAIN THERE ARE STILL CANDY MACHINES

No shadows are falling today with
no sun to drop them. You can still
buy handfuls of hard candy on certain
corners though. The rain falls
making one way, do not enter,
and yield signs out of every

mirrored window. This is not to say
that I'm lost keys, that missing sock,
or sunglasses you only find by sitting
on them—I'm just sure the sun's out

somewhere else. If I knocked on the door
of someone with a candle in their window
these days would they put me up, or out?
Politician me won't let anything
knifish come out of my mouth;
I'm becoming something of a sword

swallower. The weather glazes everything
with rain. The bodegas
that sell flowers smell better in the rain
giving me petals to use as umbrellas.

A FLOWER IN THE THROAT

The German expression *Danke fur die Blumen*
means "thanks for the compliment"
and translates as "thanks
for the flowers." Have you ever

choked on a compliment? The thing
I want to say ("Your skin reminds me of
a winter's sunset in Austria today.") would
probably get me smacked. That just accounts
for today though.

People in glass houses should close the blinds
before: sex, coffee, dinner, throwing potatoes,
or taking boudoir photos. People in glass
houses should move. I'm swallowing

all the flowers I can, but the pistils
are tough to get past my uvula. I'm afraid
one will shoot back from between my teeth
and pay itself to you who, fairly enough,
won't give me credit for an honest
thought, much less a word. ("Your eyes
remind me of the reservoir in Central Park
we saw together.")

SWEATING LIKE A TURTLE

The girl from Ipanema sweats like a turtle.
A little bead of sweat glows
on the tip of her nosey beak and sits there
like a third eye, of sorts, while she proclaims
"sometimes two eyes just aren't enough."

While proclaiming thusly
she shakes that bead right off her nose
and into the soup she's burning for lunch.
Turtles don't sweat;
I don't know the girl from Ipanema;
I burned the soup myself.

There are kids at the beach
who build sand-castles; I've seen them.
They spend hours building moats,
shaping outer walls, and
carving windows into turrets
only to knock it all down.

I've been sitting with this phenomenon,
not trying to figure it out exactly,
just acknowledging its existence.
I realized, in a brushing-my-teeth-
of-a-Tuesday-morning way,
they crush them because they made them.

THE START OF NOVEMBER, COLUMBUS CIRCLE, NEW YORK, NEW YORK

Walking to the subway after an addiction evaluation—
before getting coffee with V talking about Calvino, Hell's
Kitchen, the upcoming election, and drawing
her a diagram, my new thing,
explaining how one might create
a toy rhinoceros and another to explain
the nature of the relationship

between me and my college roommates
(Poet, Philosopher, Painter; Cucker?, Cuckold, Cuckee?;
Guy, Boyfriend, Girlfriend;
That guy, ex-boyfriend, ex-girlfriend)—
I walked through Columbus Circle and noticed,
for the first time in my three New York years,
that there are seats and a fountain in the midst of the
circle.

As I walked through a man stopped wheeling his suitcase,
took off his shoes and socks, and rolled up his trousers.
He waded into the fountain, rolled his long-sleeve-
blue-black-and-white-flannel shirt past his elbows, and
started picking out other people's dreams.

AFTER A RUSSIAN POET

I realize these minutes are short
and that the shadows
in my eyes shift as your face sets;
I wonder, though,
if you realize it as well. Secrets

are only fun if you have someone
to share them with. In spite
of all the hours I've spent reading
I've learned
to read more, or maybe better—
quality not quantity—

I also learned that pushing
your two thumbs into the stem
of an apple can put enough pressure
to split that apple in half,
and that "parity" is a word.

MISSED CONNECTIONS
A Lop-Sided Crown based on the Craigslist site of the same name

-1- Sarah

I left, as it turns out I do, for another country.
Me: skinny, gap toothed, short, with strawish-long hair
     and fourteen.
You: smiling, blonde, with the look of a French last
     name and thirteen.
I was at your house. We talked about The Beatles and
     our parents.
When I was leaving you made a banner that said "Don't
     Get Caned".
There was a cake and some kissing, something of a rabbit
thwacking someone with its ears. We cried, I told you I
     would run away.
I wouldn't have. I wanted to know my father.
When they took me away that first time, on vacation,
I wrote a letter to you once a day for two weeks.
I never mailed them, I handed them to you
in my first notebook. There was one about sunsets in
     Hong Kong
and how they reminded me of you.
If you read this get in touch; I'd like to be nearer you.

-2- Sarah

If you read this get in touch; I'd like to be nearer you.
You were my first, I was yours. Together on a beach,
when I lived in Hong Kong, after too much alcohol, pot,
        and possibly heroin
we pushed against one another trying to keep
sand away from our important parts. It didn't work.
In the morning I pissed a little piece of uncooked glass.
You smelled of Fahrenheit and smiled in two languages,
while I was still learning what women mean.
I've heard worse stories about losing your virginity,
but we were only stems then, maybe a leaf or two.
It's been 14 years and it would be fun
to see which of our edges have softened and which
        hardened.
Look for yourself, through the years, in
the mirror I'm holding up to my memory.

-3- Sarah

The mirror I'm holding up to my memory
is pivoting to catch a picture of you.
The dormouse in a high school performance
of <u>Alice in Wonderland</u>. You usually fell asleep
on my shoulder, only until the sun came up.
You had to make it back to your room for morning
bed check; after two schools neither of us wanted a third.
I made your friend cry with: "Wow, you used to be so
        pretty.
What happened?" That was the last time I saw you.
When the world decided we were unfit for daily
interactions, or needed to be retrained—we kept each
other company—a glue-trapped dormouse and her own
        mad hatter.
We've talked since those days; "Oh, you got married.
        Great.
What's he like? His name's my name?"
I just wonder what you look like now.

-4- Sarah

I just wonder what you look like now.
You had two kids and almost a third,
the third being the first (and almost mine).
The last time we kissed you said "kiss me like you mean
it; we might not see each other again." So I did and we
didn't. We told stories—razor-blades, guns,
chains, fist fights, and 63% truth. I wonder
what rainbows and car crashes
you've seen since those days.
I saw green clouds roll over your face
when I said the wrong thing
and I think I'd like to see you get mad again
almost as much as I want to sleep with you again.
You are a secret I keep almost from myself.

-5- Sarah

You were a secret I kept almost from myself;
I was the secret I kept from you. Would memory be so
durable if you knew the way I like my eggs, or all
the other girls I was making time with? You held
me together between when I realized that life wasn't for
me, and when I found one that was.
I was your first; I think your sixth is your husband.
We had moments when I didn't imagine being happier.
I know you're pregnant now and that you're happy
        without me.
You don't even have to name your first son after me
so long as we can still dance like rabbits on the phone.
I hope your husband buys you flowers more than I did.
Really, I just wanted to say congratulations on your life.

-6- Sarah

Really, I just wanted to say congratulations on your life.
We built your home together. Me with my shirt off and a
hammer in my belt; you with your shirt on and nails
        in your pouch.
We met on my twentieth birthday while I was doing gin
shots and you were "getting air," fighting with your ex-
and throwing up out the opened door of your car. I
        wondered what I was doing
with this one life and was beginning to learn *"einmal ist
        keinmal."*
I asked you to move with me; you said no because you
        were the smart one.
I went to Vermont and left you with your house,
your friends, and memories of the drunk fights we had
        on Tuesday nights.
There were things we got together, not many but
        enough to reflect starlight.
I showed you Scotland and you met my grandmother
        in Glasgow.
I wonder what you're doing and how your brother is
        coming up.
I wanted to tell you, eight years later,
I still have no idea what I'm looking for in my life.

-7- Sarah

I still have no idea what I'm looking for in this life,
but it's a point that you come up in this middle spot,
like you are more of a crisis than mid-life. We met in an
Arctic town that was either ice or mud, only rarely green.
You moved to your city and invited me to visit.
I did because I didn't know to let well enough alone.
I fell in love too and knew that sooner or later I'd live
in Manhattan. I had just learned there's more to life
than drugs and women.
Me: spiky-blonde hair, crooked smile and father issues.
You: crooked smile, dark hair and your own father
issues.
Us: wanting to say more apart in spite of having more to
say together.
The map of our feelings is mostly unexplored dark parts;
there were times enough when my eyes sang like a kite
to forget the times we shrieked like kettles.
I can't remember the words but I can still hum the tune.

-8- Sarah

I can't remember the words but I can still hum the tune
to "Leaving (on a jet plane)" and other karaoke songs.
You were my boss; I was a smarmy American.
Were there flowers there or was it just the best
kind of cultural exchange? You taught me Japanese
and made me speak like a woman. You smiled constantly
and giggled perfectly. I ran from my last Sarah as far
as the map allowed. There were snow-angels, snowball
fights, and someone's first snow-man; even if it was just
      the map's edge
there were moments worth remembering. Mostly
I remember that crows sounded different to our ears.
When I tried to tell you what crows bark like to me
and you said *"Nani?"* it tore down my little poetic
wall of misunderstanding, and the world became all
      edges and jumpers.
It was the sounds, the way we made them, that
      stopped us.

-9- Sarah

It was the sounds, the way we made them, that
        stopped us
speaking all those miles apart made it harder to hear you.
You reminded me of the home I never knew, a home-
coming of sorts. Your voice, the places it was hard
and the places it was soft, rang of home. You taught me
that, despite what the movies show, there's something
to be said for kissing with your eyes open.
Sex is sensory, sight is a sense, therefore sight
        has a place in sex.
You bought me a ticket for Korea, most of my drinks,
        and smiled so long
as we wound up in bed together. You reminded me there
        was more
to me than a quiet man in a dress shirt and tie.
You kept me speaking when everyone around me had
        different tongues,
you showed me Korea for my birthday and
I just wanted to say thank you, I guess.

-10- Sarah

I just wanted to say thank you. I guess
you won't want to hear it. For the most part though
    Ashley was right;
it looks more and more like I'll die old and alone.
I did learn to take chances without a parachute;
I also learned that because you do doesn't mean you'll
    land safely.
I moved eight hours at 300 Km/h to be with you,
on the strength of a weekend and parking-lot kisses.
It wasn't as flowery as we thought it would be but it
didn't kill us either. There are things I would do
    differently now
but as we only get one sometimes two chances at this:
    what was is.
Someone told me I ruined your idea of love. And, since
    love is nothing
but an idea, I feel like I've ruined you. Though
    that probably
gives me more power than I have. But just in case:
There are the things I would change if I could.
As nice as this might sound I was an ass.

-11- Sarah

As nice as this might sound I was an ass.
We met in Belgrade by accident and in Venice
on purpose. It was artful, or artsy, or artistic.
You asked me to come with you to Verona as you left;
I should have. I told you I didn't have my ticket. I lied.
We had our days in Venice and our night; we talked
of what little we knew about the world, each other,
and our plans. Two days in Venice and four in Belgrade.
        Those six days
have my favorite pictures, the woman on the beach,
you on the stairs that once led somewhere, but now just
        extend into space
to end in open air, like a cosmic joke. Though my
        memory is
getting blurred by time. I have four CD's and two letters
you sent me after our returns and departures—you for
        Spain, me for Austria.
I wanted to show you: it is intention, not duration, which
        matters.

-12- Sarah

I wanted to show you: it is intention, not duration, which
    matters.
We met on a train from Prague. Through a series of
happy accidents, I wound up on your doorstep a few
    weeks later.
You smiled, got me drunk with *yappee*, on your dime,
and shared your bed with me. Saying, "I could get you a
    mattress, or we could
share the bed, if you don't mind." Last I heard from you
was three years ago; you sent me a video you took of me
    at your computer
and said "this makes me smile." We talked about time
    travel and poetry.
You taught me to curse in Dutch; I taught you to count
    in Roman.
Four hours on a train, three days in Groningen,
    and all I have
to show for it is this stupid T-shirt and the memory of
    smiles
stretching your face. I wonder whether you went back to
    that frat boy.
I wonder if you're still in Groningen, or if I'd find you on
    a train.
I wonder if you're still smiling.

-13- Sarah

I wonder if you're still smiling.
I've written this before: we met in Venice, again in Paris,
once in New York, and in Montreal. There was nothing,
except the cities, that was glorious about it, which I
      realize isn't true.
At 18 you had more to say on Proust and Rimbaud
than Albertine and Verlaine would have.
This says nothing. There are questions I'd like answered.
What do you think of my new poem; did you think I
      loved her
when we met that last time; was it us or the idea
of you and me that clinched it; would you, if we lived
in the same country, see me more? What good are
      questions? What good
are more words? What do I want to say to you other than
      what I've said to you?
I'm happy and sorry we met. You made me want to smile
      like I meant it.

-14- Sarah

I'm happy and sorry we met. You made me want to smile
        like I meant it.
I've thought about the books I've read and I realized I'd
        like
to be the type who is the hero of the novel .
What sort of hero has sex with anyone
who's willing, while sharing his bed with a girl
he says he loves? Is there merit in the question
of tranquility? I don't feel oceanic now. Maybe stream,
small mildly pulsing stream, like a vein. I'm as tranquil
as a vein, as the carotid artery; I know that
I couldn't fit you comfortably between my ribs, much
        less my arms;
I know a "sorry I wasted your time" won't cut it yet.
Probably not ever, but I know there won't be a chance to
        say it again.
You: small, tattooed, smart, but not smart enough to
        really doubt me.
Me: skinnier, tattooed, smart, but not smart enough to
        know what I had.

-15- Soliloquy

If you read this get in touch; I'd like to be nearer you
        through
more than the mirror I'm holding up to my memory.
I wonder what you look like now,
you secret I kept almost from myself.
Really, I just wanted to say congratulations on your life,
I still have no idea what I'm looking for in this life.
I can't remember the words but I can still hum the tune
        to remind
me it was the sounds, the way we made them, that
        stopped us.
I just wanted to say thank you, I guess, but
as nice as this might sound I was an ass—
I wanted to show you: it is intention, not duration, which
        matters.
I wonder if you're still smiling.
I'm happy and sorry we met. You made me want to smile
        like I mean it,
and then I leave, as it turns out I do, for another country.

POSTCARDS TO _____

-5-
"Why is the heart a train station?
Why not an airport?" you might ask.
"That's more modern,
much more goes through there;
people, first kisses, new beginnings
all come through those doors."

At the airport there's no earth, no dirt, no hookers.

Ryan J. Davidson is a Scottish-American. He lives and works in New York City; he has called Hong Kong, Vermont, New Jersey, Aomori and Matsuzaka, Japan, and Graz, Austria all home. This is his first full length collection of poetry.